United States Government Accountability Office

Report to the Chairman, Committee on Homeland Security and Governmental Affairs, U.S. Senate

October 2013

2020 CENSUS

Additional Actions Could Strengthen Future Census Test Designs

GAO Highlights

Highlights of GAO-14-26, a report to the Chairman, Committee on Homeland Security and Governmental Affairs, U.S. Senate

2020 CENSUS

Additional Actions Could Strengthen Future Census Test Designs

Why GAO Did This Study

The Bureau is continuing its early testing efforts to prepare for the decennial. These tests must be well designed to produce useful information about how to implement the 2020 Census. The Bureau has completed the designs of three field tests. GAO was asked to monitor the Bureau's testing for the 2020 Census.

This report (1) determines the extent to which the Bureau followed key practices for a sound study plan in designing the earliest 2020 Decennial Census field tests, and (2) identifies what lessons were learned that may help improve future tests. To meet these objectives, GAO first selected 25 key practices for a sound research plan after reviewing its program evaluation literature. GAO then compared Bureau field test design documents for its three initial tests to these practices. GAO also examined where the Bureau had not followed key practices, identified actions needed to address them, and interviewed officials about lessons learned.

What GAO Recommends

GAO recommends that the Secretary of Commerce (1) finalize field test management revisions in the team leader handbook, (2) set a timeline and milestones for formalizing proposed field test management restructuring and guidance revisions, and (3) document lessons learned from designing initial field tests. The Department of Commerce concurred with GAO's findings and recommendations, and provided minor technical comments, which were included in the final report.

View GAO-14-26. For more information, contact Robert Goldenkoff at (202) 512-2757 or goldenkoffr@gao.gov.

What GAO Found

The Census Bureau (Bureau) generally followed most key practices for a sound study plan in designing the three initial field tests. However, some practices were only partially followed (see figure). For example, the test designs varied for four practices related to design process management. Good management of the design process can help managers identify factors that can affect the quality of a test, such as potential risk of delays and challenges to the lines of communication. For example, the Bureau generally followed one of the practices for design process management—identifying clear reporting relationships—for only one of the test designs. The Bureau partially followed this practice for another test design, and did not follow it for the third.

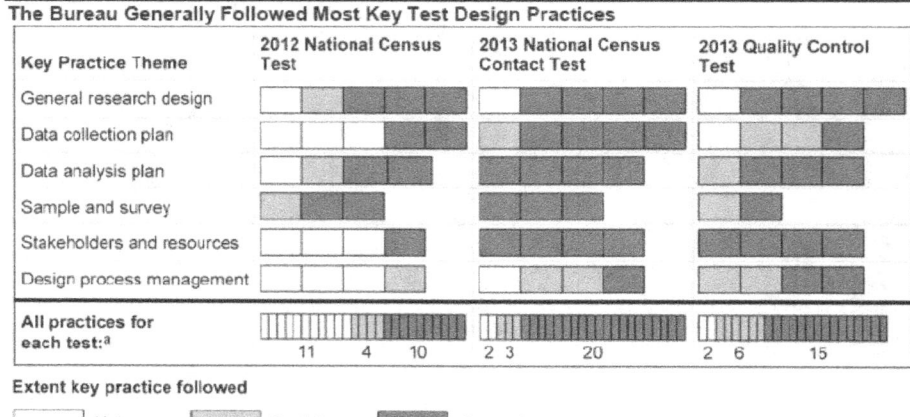

The Bureau Generally Followed Most Key Test Design Practices

Extent key practice followed: Not, Partial, Generally

Source: GAO analysis of U.S. Census Bureau data.

[a] Two of the practices are not applicable to the 2013 Quality Control Test.

The Bureau has already begun incorporating lessons learned from its initial field test designs. These lessons include obtaining internal expert review, and conducting reviews after each test to learn additional lessons. The Bureau has also recognized the importance of keeping design team leaders informed about key design elements. Yet the Bureau has not finalized planned revisions to the team leader handbook, which could help implement this lesson.

Additionally, the Bureau is realigning field test governance structures to improve communication and accountability. It has already taken such steps as identifying one point of contact for each test. However, GAO found that the Bureau needs to set timelines and milestones to formalize other restructuring proposals for managing field tests, such as creating a field test management team. Having a formalized proposal and guidance revisions will better position the Bureau to improve accountability, communication, and the monitoring of its test design processes. While lessons the Bureau identified should help it better design future field tests, it has not consistently documented these lessons learned. Documenting lessons can help reduce the risk of repeating prior deficiencies that may lead to test development delays, and can reinforce lessons learned. Given the long time frames involved in planning the census, documentation is essential to ensure lessons are incorporated into future tests.

_____ United States Government Accountability Office

Contents

Figures

Abbreviations

Bureau	U.S. Census Bureau
2013 NCCT	2012 National Census Contact Test
2012 NCT	2012 National Census Test
2013 QCT	2013 Quality Control Test

GAO

U.S. GOVERNMENT ACCOUNTABILITY OFFICE

441 G St. N.W.
Washington, DC 20548

October 25, 2013

The Honorable Thomas R. Carper
Chairman
Committee on Homeland Security and Governmental Affairs
United States Senate

Dear Mr. Chairman:

The U.S. Census Bureau (Bureau) conducts various field tests over the course of the decade to prepare for the decennial census. These tests must be designed well to produce useful information about how to implement the 2020 Census. For the 2010 Census, the Bureau conducted relatively large, infrequent, and costly field tests, which were time consuming to design, implement, and analyze. When, as a result of these tests, the Bureau needed to modify its plans or conduct additional testing, it had little time to do so. In preparation for the 2020 Census, the Bureau is designing smaller, more targeted, and less costly tests to support its decision-making process. With a total cost of about $13 billion, the 2010 Census was the costliest U.S. census in history. The Bureau is committed to limiting its per-household cost for the 2020 Census to not more than that of the estimated $94 per household cost of the 2010 Census, adjusted for inflation. It believes less costly tests can help.

You asked us to monitor the Bureau's testing for the 2020 Decennial Census. For this report, we (1) determined to what extent the Bureau followed key practices for a sound study plan in designing the earliest 2020 Decennial Census field tests, and (2) identified what lessons were learned from the design process that may help improve future tests.

To determine to what extent the Bureau followed practices for a sound study plan, we reviewed its design documents for the initial 2020 Decennial Census field tests. We also interviewed Bureau officials about the field test design process. The three tests included (1) assessing methods of providing an Internet response option, (2) measuring the accuracy of private vendor-supplied contact information, such as phone numbers and email addresses, and (3) determining how to improve quality control on mobile computing devices. We compared the Bureau's field test design documents for the three initial tests to 25 key practices from our prior work on designing evaluations, an audit of a prior Bureau census test design on overseas enumeration, and other management practices.[1] We assessed a practice as "generally followed" if the evidence showed that the Bureau followed more than 75 percent of the practice. We considered it "partially followed" if the evidence showed the Bureau followed between 25 and 75 percent of the practice, and "not followed" if the Bureau followed less than 25 percent. Our assessment provides a measure of the general rigor of the test designs. We shared these practices with the Bureau and it considered the practices reasonable. To identify lessons learned, we examined where practices had not been followed and identified corrective actions. We then discussed with Bureau officials what lessons they had learned and how the Bureau could implement them for future field tests. More information on our scope and methodology can be found in appendix I.

We conducted this performance audit from January 2013 to October 2013 in accordance with generally accepted government auditing standards. Those standards require that we plan and perform the audit to obtain sufficient, appropriate evidence to provide reasonable basis for our findings and conclusions based on our audit objectives. We believe that the evidence obtained provides a reasonable basis for our findings and conclusions based on our audit objectives.

Background

The Bureau's testing program for the 2010 Census relied principally on a small number of large-scale census-like tests. Specifically, the 2010 testing program included two national tests on the content of questionnaires in 2003 and 2005, two site tests focused on data-collection methods and systems in 2004 and 2006, and a final "dress rehearsal" at two sites in 2008. The dress rehearsal, considered to be the final step of a decade of research and testing, had the primary focus of testing automated field operations and their interfaces. The Bureau previously reported that implementing the census tests, including the dress rehearsal, cost about $108 million.

---

[1]GAO, *Designing Evaluations: 2012 Revision*, GAO-12-208G (Washington, D.C.: Jan. 2012), *2010 Census: Overseas Enumeration Test Raises Need for Clear Policy Direction*, GAO-04-470 (Washington, D.C.: May 21, 2004*), 2020 Census: Additional Steps Are Needed to Build on Early Planning*, GAO-12-626 (Washington, D.C.: May 17, 2012), *Internal Control Management and Evaluation Tool*, GAO-01-1008G (Washington, D.C.: Aug. 2001), and *Standards for Internal Control in the Federal Government*, GAO/AIMD-00-21.3.1 (Washington, D.C.: Nov. 1999).

As part of the Bureau's effort to conduct the 2020 Census at a cost lower than the 2010 Census, it plans to invest in early research and conduct smaller more frequent tests to inform its 2020 Census design decisions. The lifecycle for 2020 Census preparation is divided into five phases, as illustrated in figure 1. The Bureau is attempting to frontload critical research and testing to an earlier part of the decade than it had in prior decennials. It intends to use the early research and testing phase through fiscal year 2015 to develop a preliminary design and to evaluate the possible impact that changes would have on the census' cost and quality. By the end of the early research and testing phase, the Bureau plans to decide on preliminary operational designs.

Figure 1: Planned Research and Testing Will Help Inform Future Design Decisions

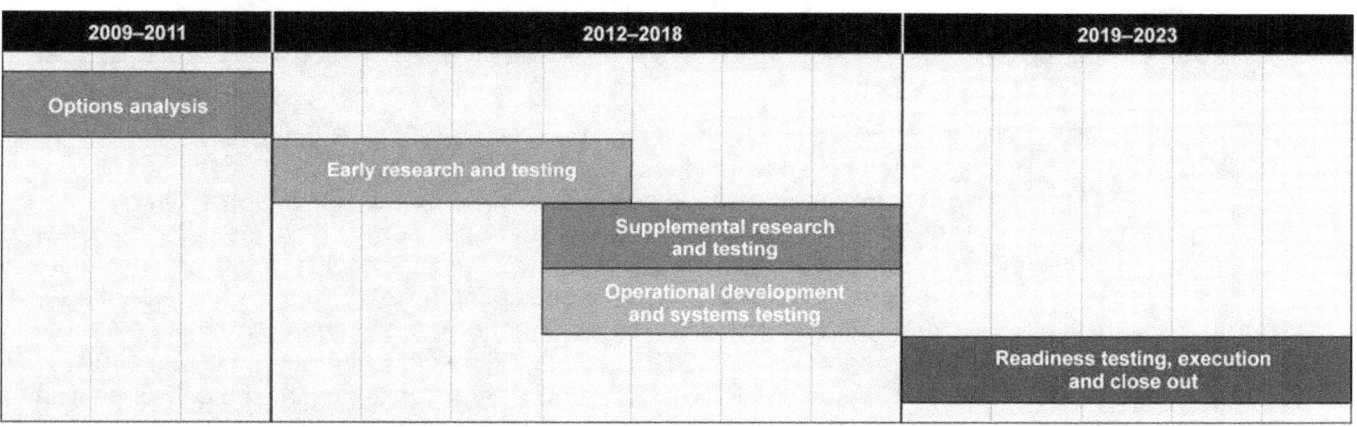

Source: GAO analysis of U.S. Census Bureau data.

In August 2012, as part of the 2020 Census testing program, the Bureau issued a research and testing management plan.[2] The plan defines eight phases of the life cycle for a census field test, as shown in figure 2. According to the plan, the first three phases culminate in the approval of a field test design by a group of senior Bureau managers that provides decision-making support to the 2020 Census program.

---

[2]U.S. Census Bureau, *2020 Census Program-Level Research and Testing Management Plan*, WBS 1.105, Version 1.0, Aug. 7, 2012.

Figure 2: Field Test Design Is Completed After First Three of Eight Life Cycle Phases

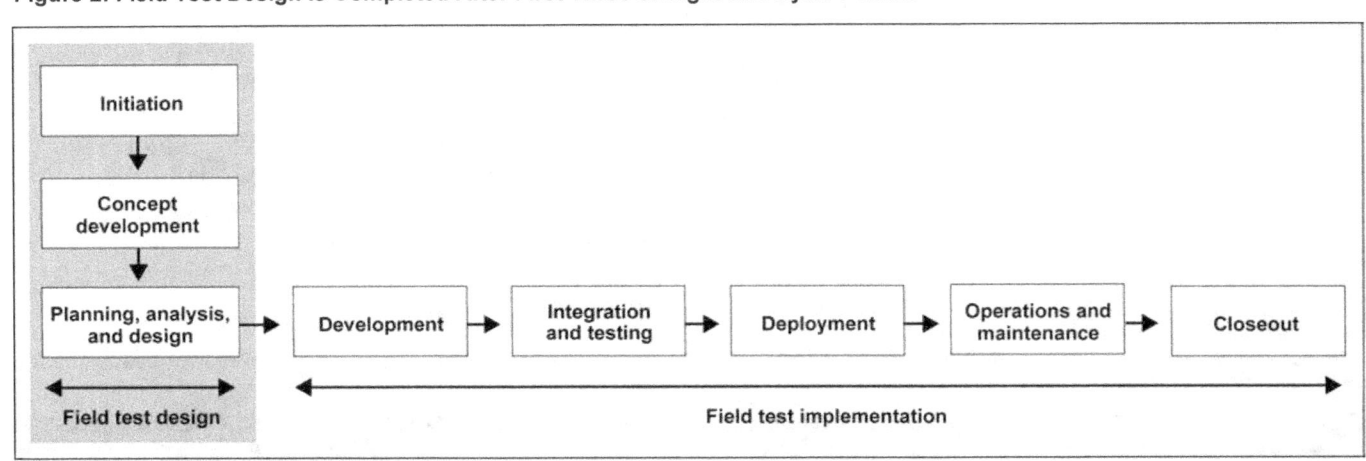

Source: GAO analysis of U.S. Census Bureau information.

To facilitate the field test design process, the Bureau developed templates as guidance for developing test designs. The Bureau also developed management plans in specific functional areas. One, a communications and stakeholder engagement plan, identified stakeholder groups involved in 2020 Census planning. Another, a governance plan, identified decision-making bodies for the 2020 Research and Testing program.[3] The plans outline processes the Bureau will implement as it prepares for the 2020 Census. Prior to this, the Bureau used 2010 Census program guidance and standards to govern some of its earliest design discussions.

The Bureau plans to conduct 10 field tests in preparation for the 2020 Census during the early research and testing phase. According to the Bureau, not all field tests are alike, and they vary in scope and capability. Some will be designed to encompass more exploratory questions. Others will be designed to more rigorously test the implementation of specific operations. When we initiated this review in early 2013, the Bureau had designed its initial three tests as summarized in table 1. Other planned field tests will cover topics such as building the address list and narrowing

[3]*United States Census 2020: 2020 Census Communications and Stakeholder Engagement Management Plan WBS 1.108*, Version 1.0, June 29, 2012 and *United States Census 2020: 2020 WBS 1.103 Governance Management Plan*, Version 0.9, Jan. 24, 2013.

possible approaches for self-response, non-response follow-up, and workload management. The field tests will culminate in a larger test late in fiscal year 2015 to further narrow possible design options.

Table 1: Summary of the Three Initial Census Field Test Designs

Test	Topics	Household sample size	Data collection method	Design completed
2012 National Census Test (2012 NCT)	Evaluate household coverage strategies on the Internet. Study the relative response rate associated with various contact strategies.	80,000	Paper Telephone Internet	August 2012
2013 National Census Contact Test (2013 NCCT)	Evaluate the quality of contact information from different vendors. Identify potential improvements for processing responses that do not have a pre-assigned tracking number.	40,000	Telephone	December 2012
2013 Quality Control Test (2013 QCT)	Research how the quality control design for operations can be improved to be more efficient and effective.	3,023	Mobile computing devices (observe how various mobile computing devices perform under scripted scenarios)	February 2013

Source: GAO analysis of U.S. Census Bureau information.

The Bureau Generally Followed Most Key Practices for Designing Tests and Has Taken Steps to Strengthen Its Design Process

Based on our prior work, we identified 25 key practices for a sound study plan. Following these practices before test designs are completed can help ensure that test designs are appropriate, feasible, and produce useful results. We organized the 25 practices into the following six themes.

- general research design,
- data collection plan,
- data analysis plan,
- sample and survey,
- stakeholders and resources, and
- design process management.

As demonstrated in figure 3, the Bureau generally followed most of the 25 key practices for two of the three field test designs and at least partially for the third field test design.

Figure 3: The Bureau Generally Followed Most Key Test Design Practices

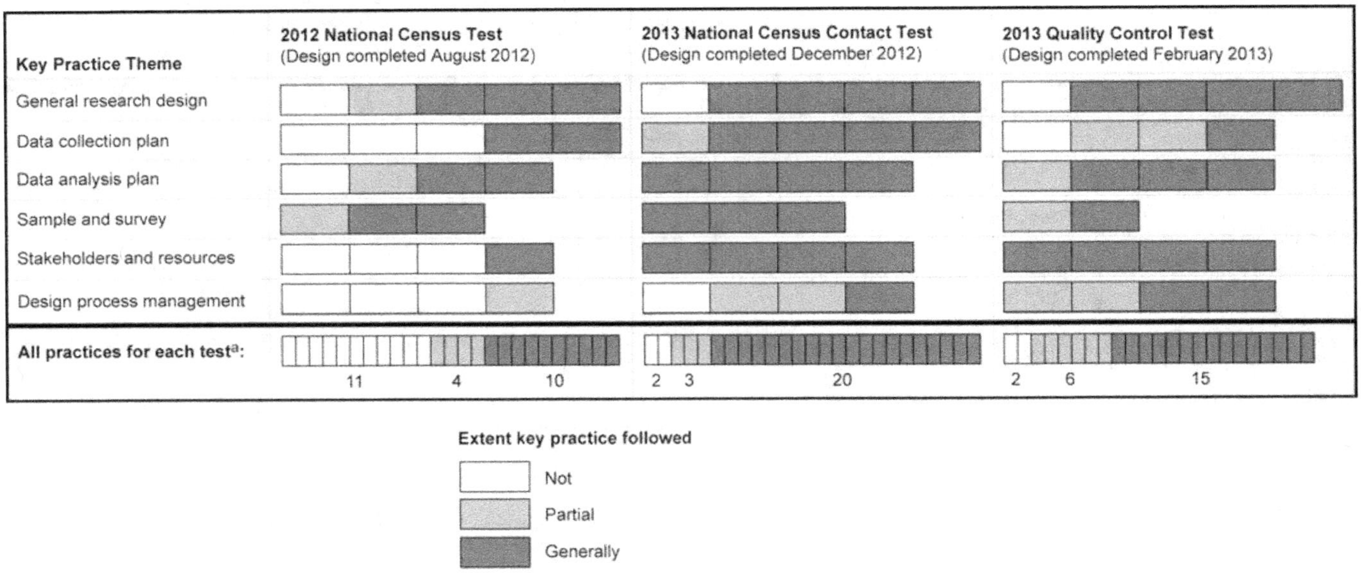

Key Practice Theme	2012 National Census Test (Design completed August 2012)	2013 National Census Contact Test (Design completed December 2012)	2013 Quality Control Test (Design completed February 2013)
General research design			
Data collection plan			
Data analysis plan			
Sample and survey			
Stakeholders and resources			
Design process management			
All practices for each test[a]:	11 4 10	2 3 20	2 6 15

Extent key practice followed

- Not
- Partial
- Generally

Source: GAO analysis of U.S. Census Bureau data.

[a]Two of the practices are not applicable to the 2013 Quality Control Test.

General Research Design

Research questions frame the scope of a test, drive the design, and help ensure that findings are useful and answer the research objectives. The objectives should be relevant, creating a clear line of sight to the Bureau's goals for the 2020 Census. In addition, clearly articulating the test design in advance of conducting a test aids researchers in discussing methodological choices with stakeholders. Across the three field tests, the Bureau generally followed three of the general research design practices, followed one practice to a varying degree, but did not follow the practice of identifying potential biases (see table 2).

Table 2: General Research Design: The Bureau Followed Most of the Practices, but Designs Did Not Address Potential Biases

Practices	Extent Followed		
	2012 National Census Test	2013 National Census Contact Test	2013 Quality Control Test
Specify objectives and questions and ensure they are linked.	◐	●	●
Ensure objectives are relevant.	●	●	●
Define concepts.	●	●	●
Identify potential biases (e.g., cultural or sample bias) and discusses how to address them.	○	○	○
Consider relevant prior research, such as census evaluations, or oversight reporting.	●	●	●

Legend: ● = generally followed, ◐ = partially followed, and ○ = not followed.

Source: GAO analysis of U.S. Census Bureau information.

The Bureau defined concepts, considered relevant prior research in each test, and included objectives that were relevant. However, the Bureau omitted research questions from the design of the 2012 National Census Test (2012 NCT). Identifying specific research questions linked to the research objectives helps ensure that answers resulting from the field test will address the needs of the 2020 Census research program reflected in the research objectives. For example, the 2013 Quality Control Test (2013 QCT) design includes an objective to investigate how the Bureau can modernize and increase the efficiency and utility of its field infrastructure. The corresponding research question states that the test will research the feasibility of using Global Positioning System (GPS) data. The test would determine, among other things, if field staff appropriately visited housing units for address listing and enumeration and if GPS data can be used to reduce or eliminate field quality control checks. None of the three test designs addressed potential biases, such as cultural bias. If a test design does not address potential biases, systematic errors could be introduced. Such errors could affect the accuracy of the test and thus potential design decisions for the 2020 Census.

Data Collection Plan

Identifying data sources and data collection procedures is key to obtaining relevant and credible information. The Bureau generally followed two of the data collection practices for all three tests and followed the others to varying degrees (see table 3).

Table 3: Data Collection Plan: The Bureau Generally Followed the Practice of Stating How to Collect Data and Encourage Responses, but Followed Other Practices to Varying Degrees

Practices	Extent Followed		
	2012 National Census Test	2013 National Census Contact Test	2013 Quality Control Test
Clearly state how data will be collected.	●	●	●
Discuss a plan for administering and monitoring data collection.	○	●	◐
Identify and explain the level of difficulty in obtaining the data.	○	◐	◐
Identify factors that may interfere with data collection.	○	●	○
Identify a method to encourage responses.	●	●	N/A[a]

Legend: ● = generally followed, ◐ = partially followed, and ○ = not followed.

Source: GAO analysis of U.S. Census Bureau information.

[a]Because this test tested quality control functions and did not survey respondents, this practice is not applicable.

In its initial three field test designs, the Bureau generally followed the practices of clearly presenting how data will be collected, and describing a method to encourage responses, as applicable. The three other practices were followed less consistently. These practices help researchers ensure that the data collected for a test will be sufficient and appropriate. First, only the 2013 National Census Contact Test (2013 NCCT) design included a plan for administering and monitoring data collection. The test designs should include data collection procedures that will obtain relevant and credible information to ensure that the resulting information meets the decision maker's needs. In its design documents, Bureau officials explained they would collect data using telephone interviews from Census Bureau contact centers, outbound interviewing, and telephone questionnaire assistance. The Bureau further explained that survey data and the information on the outcomes of calls would be provided to the survey team. Second, the Bureau discussed the level of difficulty in two of the test designs, but did not explain why it would be difficult to obtain the data. Bureau officials stated that with limited resources and based on the importance of the objectives of a given test, they will not be able to apply all the practices equally to every test design. For example, the 2013 QCT relied on tests of software by Bureau staff— not a traditional field test involving contact with households. So, although the Bureau identified that it may be difficult to reliably identify deviations in procedures using GPS, it did not include an explanation or mitigation of the possible difficulty. Third, the Bureau only identified factors that may interfere with data collection in the 2013 NCCT design.

Data Analysis Plan

Pre-specifying a data analysis plan as part of a test design can help researchers select the most appropriate data to measure and the most accurate and reliable ways to collect them. Although the Bureau generally followed two of the four practices related to a data analysis plan in the test designs that we reviewed, its discussion of the possible limitations of findings or test results varied (see table 4).

Table 4: Data Analysis Plan: The Bureau Generally Followed Two of the Practices, but Discussion of Limitations of Findings Varied

Practices	Extent Followed		
	2012 National Census Test	2013 National Census Contact Test	2013 Quality Control Test
Identify proposed techniques for analysis.	◕	●	●
Identify how a basis for comparing the results of the research will be provided.	●	●	●
Discusses the possible limitations of the findings or test results.	○	●	◕
Proposed design or research plan is directly related to the objectives and/or questions.	●	●	●

Legend: ● = generally followed, ◕ = partially followed, and ○ = not followed.

Source: GAO analysis of U.S. Census Bureau information.

For all of the test designs, the Bureau generally identified a basis for comparing the test results and included a proposed design or research plan that was directly related to the objectives and/or questions. In addition, analytical techniques were proposed for two of three of the test designs. While in the 2012 NCT design the Bureau documented that the information from re-interviewing respondents will be used to validate their initial responses, officials did not discuss how they would match this information. Lastly, only the 2013 NCCT design included a discussion of possible limitations. For example, in its design the Bureau noted that one of the data sources used in the test might not be representative. Discussing possible limitations is important so that it is clear what the test design can and cannot address, and so that test results are not overly generalized.

Sample and Survey

A survey with an appropriate sample design can provide descriptive information about a population and its subgroups, as well as information about relationships among variables being measured. In addition, researchers should consult prior relevant research and test any new questions so that the survey questions will elicit appropriate information from respondents to address the Bureau's data needs. For all three tests, the Bureau generally followed two of the sample and survey practices, while use of the third practice varied across the field tests (see table 5).

Table 5: Sample and Survey Practices: The Bureau Generally Followed Two Practices, but Did Not Consistently Provide a Rationale for Sample Size

Practices	Extent Followed		
	2012 National Census Test	2013 National Census Contact Test	2013 Quality Control Test
Identify the sample and discuss how to reach the intended sample.	●	●	●
Explain the rationale for the size and type of sample.	◐	●	◐
Discuss the status of the survey instrument or questionnaire, with mention of prior or planned testing or related research.	●	●	N/A[a]

Legend: ● = generally followed and ◐ = partially followed.

Source: GAO analysis of U.S. Census Bureau information.

[a]Because this test tested quality control functions and did not survey respondents, this practice is not applicable.

Across the test designs, the Bureau included both a discussion of how to reach the intended sample and the status of the survey instrument or questionnaire, as applicable. While all of the test designs included a rationale for the type of sample, the 2013 NCCT design also included a rationale for the size of its sample. Bureau documents showed this sample size was selected due to the absence of any documentation of a prior study and the test team's conservative estimation of the response rate. Further, the Bureau noted the estimated response rate and selected sample size needed to enable the team to determine the quality and comprehensiveness of the data in its analysis. Test designs that explain how their sampling methodology will yield information of sufficient quality for its intended purpose provide a better justification for their cost.

Stakeholders and Resources

Managing stakeholders, identifying team member responsibilities, and identifying resources are key to a test's success, as people are the primary resource of a high-performing organization. For the 2013 test designs, the Bureau followed all of the stakeholder and resource practices. The 2012 test design did not follow three of the four practices (see table 6).

Table 6: Stakeholders and Resources: For the 2013 Test Designs, the Bureau Generally Followed All of the Practices, but the 2012 Test Design Generally Followed Only One Practice

Practices	Extent Followed		
	2012 National Census Test	2013 National Census Contact Test	2013 Quality Control Test
Identify proposed time and resources.	●	●	●
Identify stakeholders and their respective roles.	○	●	●
Discuss how stakeholders were involved in the planning or review of the methods of data collection.	○	●	●
Identify roles and responsibilities for individuals, units, or both, who are responsible for preparing the design.	○	●	●

Legend: ● = generally followed and ○ = not followed.

Source: GAO analysis of U.S. Census Bureau information.

The Bureau included a timeline and required resources in each field test design, including how much each field test would cost. The Bureau also generally followed the other practices related to stakeholders and resources for two of the test designs. However, for the 2012 NCT, officials did not identify stakeholders, their respective roles in the test, or their involvement in developing the test design. The latter two tests were designed with management plans for communication, stakeholder engagement, and governance, which for example, states that stakeholders' roles should be defined and that their feedback should be gathered. The 2013 Quality Census Test design documented the role that a stakeholder had in outlining how the Bureau can increase data accuracy. By including these practices in guidance, the Bureau has better ensured that its people and resources are being effectively and efficiently leveraged during the development of future 2020 Census tests.

Design Process Management

Good management of the design process can help managers identify factors that can affect test quality, such as potential risk of delays and challenges to the lines of communication. Across the three tests, the Bureau's governance process for developing test designs varied in following the four practices (see table 7).

Table 7: Design Process Management: The Bureau Followed Four Practices to Varying Degrees

Practices	Extent Followed		
	2012 National Census Test	2013 National Census Contact Test	2013 Quality Control Test
Identify clear internal reporting relationships including who reports to whom and points of contact for different types of information.	○	◓	●
Identify review and approval roles related to the management of the design process.	○	●	●
Identify performance measures and how they will be monitored.	◓	◓	◓
Clearly document approval of test design.	○	○	◓

Legend: ● = generally followed, ◓ = partially followed, and ○ = not followed.

Source: GAO analysis of U.S. Census Bureau information.

First, the Bureau identified clear reporting relationships for only the 2013 QCT. It partially followed this practice for the 2013 NCCT design, and did not follow it for the 2012 NCT design. For the two latter tests, the Bureau utilized membership lists and responsibilities matrices to identify test and project teams, and the assigned tasks and deliverables. Second, the Bureau identified review and approval roles for two of the test designs, but not for the 2012 NCT. For example, for the 2013 QCT design, the Bureau identified which individuals were supposed to review and approve certain design documents. When authority is clearly assigned and communicated, individuals can be held responsible accordingly.

Third, the Bureau's documentation of performance measures and timelines with associated milestones for all three test designs did not identify how the measures would be monitored. For example, for the 2013 QCT design the Bureau included a list of deliverables with associated dates, such as sending an initial study plan to senior Bureau officials for their review. However, it did not indicate how the Bureau would know whether these deliverables were implemented by the indicated dates. Measuring and monitoring performance allows Bureau managers to track progress toward their goals and have crucial information on which to base their organizational and management decisions.

Fourth, the Bureau did not follow its guidance for approving its 2013 NCCT test design and only partially followed it for the 2013 QCT design. According to the Bureau's August 2012 research and testing management plan, the test designs should be approved at four different stages. The test design phase is complete after the fourth approval. The

Bureau partially followed this practice for the 2013 QCT by documenting approval of its design at only one of the stages. According to Bureau meeting records, senior Bureau officials discussed the 2013 NCCT design after its implementation. Further, Bureau records indicate that senior Bureau officials discussed the 2012 NCT design, before the August 2012 management plan was issued, but did not document approval. In July 2013, the Bureau began using a table that includes test-design approval dates. This practice helps ensure that management's approval of a plan maintains its relevance and value to management in control over operations. Further, documenting that management has approved a design provides accountability and offers transparency as to when decisions were made.

Recent Changes to a Design Template Could Help the Bureau Better Follow Key Practices in Future Test Designs

The Bureau's design templates outline the information that should be included in two of its key design documents, the field test overview and the field test plan. The templates list topics to be discussed in the overview and plan, and, in some cases, provide examples of what staff should include for a topic. We found that the templates did not address some of the practices we identified for a sound study plan. For example, the templates did not require a test design to include (1) discussion of potential biases, (2) identification of factors that could interfere with obtaining data, (3) identification of difficulties in collecting data, and (4) specification of stakeholder's roles. In response to this audit, the Bureau subsequently revised its field test template to include these four practices as topics to be discussed.

The Bureau Has Already Begun Incorporating Lessons Learned from Initial Test Designs

As the Bureau works to develop field tests to inform decisions about the 2020 Census, Bureau officials are learning lessons that can strengthen the design of future tests. According to Bureau officials, our audit helped to reinforce the Bureau's need to draw on early lessons learned from initial tests. These lessons were derived from examining where the Bureau did not follow best practices for study designs and identifying corrective actions. The Bureau has adopted some of these test design lessons and is taking steps to adopt others. Table 8 lists six lessons learned from the initial three field tests.

Table 8: Lessons Learned from the Bureau's Initial Field Tests

- Involve management early in the test development process to obtain buy-in of test objectives, scope, and methodology
- Present design plans, samples, and objectives for field tests to Bureau-wide expert research and testing panel prior to conducting the test
- Conduct post-test reviews after developing each test
- Track the status of field test design deliverables across all tests
- Ensure team leaders are informed of key design elements
- Maintain reporting structures that support clear communication

Source: GAO analysis of U.S. Census Bureau information.

Obtain Management Buy-in Early

One lesson the Bureau identified is the importance of obtaining buy-in from management early in the test development process. While designing the three initial tests, Bureau field test designers did not brief senior Bureau management on the development of the designs or involve them in the planning or review of data collection methods. In addition, managers of various Bureau divisions responsible for methodology and other subject matter areas requested to be involved in the process earlier. According to Bureau officials, without early involvement, it may be difficult to obtain upper management approval of test designs quickly, which can lead to unexpected late changes or delays in testing. Early managerial involvement can help ensure early agreement on goals, objectives, timing, and capabilities needed to support a test. This lesson complements the practices of identifying stakeholders benefiting from the field test as well as stakeholders involved in the preparation of the design.

To involve management earlier, Bureau officials began briefing upper management about the planning of tests during other regularly scheduled agency-wide executive meetings early in the test planning stages. Officials also started conducting one-day planning sessions beginning with tests planned for fiscal year 2014. Since beginning these sessions, Bureau officials said they have improved at communicating input from external experts at the National Academy of the Sciences to upper Bureau management. Further, officials said they have found the sessions to be effective in identifying issues early. Bureau officials said they now intend to hold these planning sessions for each test.

Obtain Internal Expert Review

In January 2013, the Bureau began convening a Bureau-wide test strategy review body. This panel of experts first met after the 2013 National Census Contact Test was implemented. In February 2013, Bureau officials decided that prior to conducting future tests, design teams would present the plans, sample design, and objectives to the panel. According to the Bureau, the panel will now look at the Bureau's research strategy and goals, design decisions, and how the field tests will affect design decisions in fiscal years 2014 and 2015, and clarify operational milestones. The first pre-implementation presentation was conducted in February 2013 for the 2013 Quality Control Test. This allowed the test team to clarify the 2013 QCT's purpose and verify its testing methodology with Bureau-wide experts. Bureau research managers believe the test's design is better because of these meetings, and expect future test designs to benefit similarly.

Conduct Post-Test Reviews

During our review, we discussed with Bureau officials whether the Bureau took steps to evaluate the test development process after the three initial tests. The officials told us they recently started conducting staff reviews of tests they have implemented. Such post-test reviews allow the Bureau the opportunity to identify any further lessons learned from developing tests to improve either the design or management of remaining tests for the 2020 Census. The Bureau conducted its first post-test review following the 2013 National Census Contact Test. The review documented, for example, that involving stakeholders such as methodologists, in test planning and identifying their roles and responsibilities helps improve communication during the design process. Further, the review documented that test designs should not only identify responsible parties, but have information on what deliverables are expected of these parties. In addition, the Bureau also conducted a review of the 2013 Quality Control Test. Going forward, these reviews will provide the Bureau with additional opportunities to build its knowledge base on conducting small, targeted field tests.

Track the Status of Field Test Design Deliverables Across All Tests

The Bureau has taken steps to improve how it monitors the status of field test design deliverables. Bureau officials said that they previously reported on the status of some test deliverables in a biweekly report. However, these reports did not track the status of all deliverables across all the tests. As a result, senior decennial managers had to contact individual test team leaders to obtain the status for each of the initial test designs. Bureau officials acknowledged that our review led them to realize that with additional field test designs being created, monitoring across all field tests would improve their test status reporting process, and increase their efficiency in collating status information for managers. In July 2013, a Bureau official informed us that they began using a new tracking sheet to monitor the progress of field test deliverables. The new tracking tool provides a more comprehensive and global perspective on the status of deliverables across all tests. Bureau officials described this as an evolving process and said that they plan to take additional steps to develop a process for monitoring the status of field tests as well.

Ensure Team Leaders Are Informed of Key Design Elements

The Bureau has also recognized the importance of keeping team leaders informed about key design elements. According to the Bureau, design teams are required to submit certain documents for field test design reviews and approvals. Testing guidance is available electronically. Newly assigned team leaders are individually emailed links to baseline documents. New team leaders are also provided a team leader handbook. However, the handbook does not identify which documents are required for field test design development, nor does it indicate which documents were required for submission for test design reviews or approvals. Without having a listing of required documents, the Bureau risks duplicating its efforts to keep team leaders informed of key design elements. To ensure that team leaders are consistently informed of field test development guidance and the documents that should be prepared to support test design reviews and approvals, Bureau officials said they plan to include a listing of such documents in the team leader handbook. Bureau officials acknowledged that our work offered a way of improving how some information is disseminated to team leaders. The effort to revise the team leader handbook is in progress, but Bureau officials could not provide a timeline for completing it. Achieving a consistent understanding among team leaders of documents required for field test design approvals could help reduce possible delays in the test design review process.

Maintain Reporting Structures That Support Clear Communication

In response to this audit and as part of its effort to adapt its management structures to oversee multiple census field tests being developed concurrently, Bureau officials say that they are realigning field test governance processes to improve communication and accountability. Further, they said that the Bureau has already taken steps to identify one point of contact for each future test. Previously, a field test coordinator had to track input from various project team leaders involved with a particular census field test. This lesson complements the practice of identifying clear internal reporting relationships, including who reports to whom and points of contact for different types of information for a sound research plan. In addition to identifying reporting relationships, the Bureau acknowledged that taking steps like establishing one point of contact will help it to more effectively maintain clear lines of communication, and establish accountability when it develops a field test.

While the Bureau has taken some initial steps to implement its proposed restructuring, such as conducting a field test management group meeting to further integrate the 2020 field tests across projects, it has not formalized other proposed field test management restructuring and guidance revisions. For example, to improve the coordination of field test planning, the Bureau has proposed creating a field test management team that would provide centralized coordination and streamline the test processes. Further, Bureau officials said that the research and testing plan is under review and being updated to reflect the current process for approving field test designs and plans. Internal controls require that agencies complete, within established time frames, all actions that correct or otherwise resolve the matters brought to management's attention. The controls also require management to periodically evaluate the organizational structure and make changes as necessary in response to changing conditions. But, the proposed restructuring and guidance revisions have not yet been formalized. The Bureau has many other competing priorities that may need attention more urgently and officials could not provide us a timeline or milestones for formalizing the changes. Meanwhile, the Bureau is continuing work on the design of tests. Without a timeline and milestones for this restructuring, the Bureau risks uncoordinated management for its field tests. This puts the field test's effectiveness and efficiency regarding possible overlap and duplication at risk.

Lastly, it is important for the Bureau to document the lessons it has learned from designing its initial tests. In conducting post-test reviews, the Bureau documented some lessons learned from the 2013 National Census Contact Test and 2013 Quality Control Test. However, Bureau officials acknowledged that the Bureau did not consistently document the lessons learned from the design phases for the initial tests. Internal controls require that managers use control activities, such as the production of records or documentation, to aid in managing risk. Documenting these lessons can help reduce the risk of repeating prior deficiencies or inconsistencies that may lead to test development delays. Given the long time frames involved in planning the census, documentation is essential to ensure lessons are incorporated into future tests.

Conclusion

In its effort to design smaller and more targeted tests for the 2020 Census, the Bureau has taken important steps that could make its testing strategy more effective. The Bureau's investments in early testing are intended to validate the use of strategies and innovations geared toward reducing cost. The three test designs we reviewed generally or partially followed most key practices for designing a sound research plan. The Bureau has already begun taking corrective actions on others, in part by adding additional requirements for designs to its standard guidance. Finalizing planned revisions that focus on field test management in the team leader handbook can help improve how team leaders learn about test design elements. Formalizing its proposed field test management restructuring and guidance revisions will enable the Bureau to ensure that there is improved accountability, communication, and monitoring of its test management design processes. Further, documenting lessons learned while designing the initial field tests can increase the Bureau's ability to take advantage of the prior experiences. By ensuring these practices are consistently used in field tests, the Bureau will increase the soundness of the tests in areas such as design management and stakeholder involvement. This, in turn, will enhance the likelihood that the Bureau achieves its goal of conducting a cost effective census.

Recommendation for Executive Action

We recommend that the Secretary of Commerce require the Under Secretary for Economic Affairs who oversees the Economics and Statistics Administration, as well as the Director of the U.S. Census Bureau, to take the following three steps to improve the Bureau's process of designing its census field tests for the 2020 Census:

- Finalize planned revisions that focus on field test management in the team leader handbook.
- Set a timeline and milestones for formalizing proposed field test management restructuring and guidance revisions.
- Document lessons learned from designing initial field tests.

Agency Comments and Our Evaluation

We provided a draft of this report to the Department of Commerce for comment. In its written comments, reproduced in appendix II, the Department of Commerce concurred with our recommendations. The Department of Commerce also provided minor technical comments that were incorporated, as appropriate. As agreed with your offices, unless you publicly announce the contents of this report earlier, we plan no further distribution until 30 days from the report date. At that time, we will send copies to the Secretary of Commerce, the Under Secretary of Economic Affairs, the Director of the U.S. Census Bureau, and interested congressional committees. In addition, the report will be available at no charge on GAO's website at http://www.gao.gov.

If you or your staff have any questions about this report please contact me at (202) 512-2757 or goldenkoffr@gao.gov. Contact points for our Offices of Congressional Relations and Public Affairs may be found on the last page of this report. The GAO staff that made major contributions to this report is listed in appendix III.

Sincerely yours,

Robert Goldenkoff
Director
Strategic Issues

Appendix I: Objectives, Scope, and Methodology

The objectives of our review were to determine to what extent the Bureau followed key practices for a sound study plan in designing the earliest 2020 Decennial Census field tests, and to identify any lessons learned from the design process that may help improve future tests. To identify key practices for a sound study plan, we reviewed program evaluation literature, including our design evaluation guide, our 2004 review of Census Bureau overseas field tests, our 2012 review of the planning of the 2020 Census, and our guide to internal controls.[1]

We selected 25 key practices from these sources. We shared these practices with the Bureau and it agreed that they were reasonable. Using these criteria, we evaluated whether the Bureau's three initial field test designs followed key practices for a sound research plan. Additionally, since the program evaluation literature noted the importance of program management to developing a sound study plan, we also interviewed Bureau officials on the management processes used for developing the designs. We did not evaluate the outcomes of the field tests.

To determine to what extent the designs for the initial 2020 Decennial Census field tests were consistent with key practices for a sound study plan, we reviewed Bureau design documents and interviewed Bureau officials about the field test design process. We compared each of the 25 practices to the Bureau's field test design documents for the three initial tests to answer the question of whether the respective practice was followed. Our determinations provide a measure of the general rigor of the test designs, although they do not recognize the extent to which the Bureau may have considered the key practices later in the life cycle of the designs.

After comparing documents provided by the Bureau for each field test to the key practices and determining the extent each practice was followed for each test, we verified the determinations by having different auditors independently determine the extent practices were followed for 25 percent of each others' initial determinations for each test. We rated each

---

[1]GAO, *Designing Evaluations: 2012 Revision*, GAO-12-208G (Washington, D.C.: Jan. 2012), *2010 Census: Overseas Enumeration Test Raises Need for Clear Policy Direction*, GAO-04-470 (Washington, D.C.: May 21, 2004*), 2020 Census: Additional Steps Are Needed to Build on Early Planning*, GAO-12-626 (Washington, D.C.: May 17, 2012), *Internal Control Management and Evaluation Tool*, GAO-01-1008G (Washington, D.C.: Aug. 2001), and *Standards for Internal Control in the Federal Government*, GAO/AIMD-00-21.3.1 (Washington, D.C.: Nov. 1999).

practice as being either "generally followed," "partially followed," or "not followed." We also discussed our preliminary findings with Bureau officials to learn of additional context or documents that we might have missed. Table 9 describes how we made our determinations.

Table 9: Definitions of the Extent to Which Bureau Test Designs Followed Key Practices

Assessment	Definition
Generally Followed	The Bureau's test design documents indicate that the practice was considered generally followed at that time. A practice was considered generally followed when, allowing for some level of ambiguity, the evidence demonstrates that the Bureau generally followed more than 75 percent of the practice.
Partially Followed	The Bureau's test design documents indicate that only selected portions of the practice were followed at that time. A practice was considered partially followed when, allowing for some level of ambiguity, the evidence demonstrates that the Bureau followed between 25 to 75 percent of the practice.
Not Followed	The Bureau's test design documents indicate that the Bureau followed less than 25 percent of the practice, or that no evidence of it having been followed exists. A practice was considered not followed when, allowing for some level of ambiguity, the evidence indicated (1) none of the elements of the practice were evident, or (2) less than 25 percent of the practice was followed.

Source: GAO

For each test, we limited our scope to the "design" of the tests, which is the first three of eight phases of the field test life cycle and includes initiation, concept development, and planning, analysis and design.

Our reviews of test designs were designed as snapshots "as of" the approval of the designs by senior management, or at an equivalent stage of their life cycle, intended to benchmark or baseline the preparation of future test designs. As such, our determination that a given test design did not follow a given key practice does not mean that the Bureau did not consider that key practice later in the test's life cycle.

To identify lessons learned from how the tests were designed, we examined where the Bureau had not followed key practices and identified corrective actions needed. We determined the extent to which the key practice criteria were followed and then considered whether there was a pattern or an underlying cause, such as a lack of guidance. We then discussed with Bureau officials what lessons they had learned and what lessons they could implement for future field tests.

We conducted this performance audit from January 2013 to October 2013 in accordance with generally accepted government auditing standards. Those standards require that we plan and perform the audit to obtain sufficient, appropriate evidence to provide reasonable basis for our findings and conclusions based on our audit objectives. We believe that

the evidence obtained provides a reasonable basis for our findings and
conclusions based on our audit objectives.

Appendix II: Comments from the Department of Commerce

THE DEPUTY SECRETARY OF COMMERCE
Washington, D.C. 20230

September 30, 2013

Mr. Robert Goldenkoff
Director
Strategic Issues
United States Government Accountability Office
Washington, DC 20548

Dear Mr. Goldenkoff:

The U.S. Department of Commerce appreciates the opportunity to comment on the United States Government Accountability Office's draft report titled *2020 Census: Additional Actions Could Strengthen Future Census Test Designs* (GAO-14-26). The Department's comments on this report are enclosed.

Sincerely,

Patrick Gallagher
Acting Deputy Secretary of Commerce

Enclosure

U.S. Department of Commerce
Comments on the
United States Government Accountability Office
Draft Report titled, *2020 Census: Additional Actions Could Strengthen
Future Census Test Designs*
GAO-14-26
October 2013

The U.S. Census Bureau appreciates the opportunity to review this draft report. We have no substantive comments or disagreements with the findings in this report, and we welcome the suggestions and recommendations for improvements to our future 2020 Census test design efforts.

However, we do have one editorial comment for the bottom of page 19. It refers to the Acting Secretary of Commerce and Acting Director of the Census Bureau. We no longer have acting officials in these positions, but now have both a Secretary and Director.

Appendix III: GAO Contact and Staff Acknowledgments

GAO Contact	Robert Goldenkoff, (202) 512-2757 or goldenkoffr@gao.gov
Staff Acknowledgments	In addition to the contact named above, Ty Mitchell, Assistant Director; Maya Chakko; Robert Gebhart; Ellen Grady, Wilfred Holloway; Andrea Levine; Donna Miller; and Aku Pappoe made key contributions to this report.